The Kiss

The Kiss

A JAMBALAYA

John Frederick Nims

HOUGHTON MIFFLIN COMPANY BOSTON
1982

Library of Congress Cataloging in Publication Data

Nims, John Frederick, date
    The kiss.

    I. Title.
PS3527.I863K5   811'.54   81-7111
ISBN 0-395-31829-7   AACR2
ISBN 0-395-31830-0 (pbk.)

Printed in the United States of America

Q 10 9 8 7 6 5 4 3 2 1

ACKNOWLEDGMENTS

Grateful acknowledgment is made to the editors of the following magazines, in which these poems, sometimes in earlier versions or under other titles, first appeared: "Emily, Alison: Julie. And Joan," in *The American Scholar;* "Love Song for Outer Space," "Daughter, Age 4," "A Ballad of Kisses and Combs," and "How to Tell the Girls from the Flowers," *Chicago Tribune Magazine;* "The Observatory Ode," *Harvard Magazine;* "Plaza de Toros" and "Tide Turning," *The Atlantic Monthly;* "A Song of the Poet H'i Hsi" and "Sonnet Almost Petrarchan," *Sewanee Review;* "The Year 1520" and "Spleen" ("Catullus lxx"), *The Saturday Review.* The poem "Love and Death" first appeared in *Of Flesh and Bone* (Rutgers University Press, 1967).

The author is also grateful to the following for permission to reprint certain poems: "Advice from the Classics," from *Sappho to Valéry: Poems in Translation* by John Frederick Nims; copyright © 1971 by John Frederick Nims; published by Princeton University Press (Princeton Paperback, 1980); reprinted by permission of Princeton University Press. "Back to Basics," *The Little Magazine,* Fall 1977 (copyright 1978). "A Scholar Wonders" (copyright © 1973 by the Modern Poetry Association) and "Cardiological" (copyright © 1977 by the

With a kiss for Bonnie, Sally, and Emily

Béseme de besos de su boca, porque buenos
tus amores más que el vino.

Fray Luis de León, *El Cantar de Cantares*

CONTENTS

The Kiss

THE OBSERVATORY ODE
Harvard, June 1978

I

The Universe:
We'd like to understand,
But any piece, in the palm, gets out of hand,
Any stick, any stone,
— How mica burns! — or worse,
Any star we catch in pans of glass,
Sift to a twinkle the vast nuclear zone,
Lava-red, polar-blue,
Apple-gold (noon our childhood knew),
Colors that through the prism, like dawn through Gothic, pass,
Or in foundries sulk among grots and gnomes, in glare
of zinc or brass.
Would Palomar's flashy cannon say? Would you,
Old hourglass, galaxy of sand,
You, the black hole where Newton likes to stand?

II

Once on this day,
Our Victorian renaissance-man,
Percival Lowell — having done Japan,
And soon to be seen
Doing over all heaven his way —
Spoke poems here. (These cheeks, a mite
Primped by the laurel leaves' symbolical green,
Should glow like the flustered beet
To scuff, in his mighty shoes, these feet.)
He walked high ground, each long cold Arizona night,
Grandeurs he'd jot: put folk on Mars, but guessed a planet right,
Scribbling dark sums and ciphers at white heat
For his Pluto, lost. Till — there it swam!
Swank, with his own P L for monogram.

III

Just down the way
The Observatory. And girls
Attending, with lint of starlight in their curls,
To lens, 'scope, rule.
Sewing bee, you could say:
They stitch high heaven together here,
Save scraps of the midnight sky. Compile, poll, pool.
One, matching star with star,
Learns that *how bright* can mean *how far.*
That widens the galaxies! Each spiraling chandelier
In three-dimensional glamour hangs; old flat nights disappear.
Desk-bound, they explore the immensities. Who are
These women that, dazed at dusk, arise?
— No Helen with so much heaven in her eyes.

IV

With what good night
Did the strange women leave?
What did the feverish planet-man achieve?
A myth for the sky:
All black. Then a haze of light,
A will-o'-the-wisp, hints *time* and *place*.
Whirling, the haze turned fireball, and let fly
Streamers of bright debris,
The makings of our land and sea.
Great rafts of matter crash, their turbulence a base
For furnaces of nuclear fire that blast out slag in space.
Primal pollution, dust and soot, hurl free
Lead, gold — all that. Heaven's gaudy trash.
This world — with our joy in June — is a drift of ash.

V

That fire in the sky
On the Glorious Fourth, come dark,
Acts "Birth of the Universe" out, in Playland Park.
Then a trace of ash
In the moon. Suppose we try
— Now only suppose — to catch in a jar
That palmful of dust, on bunsens burn till it flash,
Could we, from that gas aglow,
Construct the eventful world we know,
Or a toy of it, in the palm? Yet our world came so: we are
Debris of a curdled turbulence, and dust of a dying star
— The children of nuclear fall-out long ago.
No wonder if late world news agree
With Eve there's a creepy varmint in the Tree.

VI

The Universe:
. . . Such stuff as dreams are made on . . .
Yet stuff to thump, to call a spade a spade on.
No myth — Bantu,
Kurd, Urdu, Finnish, Erse —
Had for the heaven such hankering
As ours, that made new eyes for seeing true.
For seeing what we are:
Sun-bathers of a nuclear star,
Scuffing through curly quarks — mere fact a merry thing!
Then let's, with the girls and good P.L., sing carols in a ring!
Caution: combustible myth, though. Near and far
The core's aglow. No heat like this,
No heat like science and poetry when they kiss.

IN GREEK OF BYZANTIUM

. . . Penzias and Wilson had detected a weak background radio signal that came equally from all directions in space at a wavelength of 7.35 centimeters, a phenomenon that they could not then explain . . .

How all began here? For a start, we go
To that first of the gorgeous make-believings, no?
". . . Took clay . . . breathed in a soul . . ." So *Genesis.*
Breathed
— on His scruffy nude? —
the nuclear kiss.

What thunder and flare! What lava! Cataclysms!
Madness in magnets! And
— wildfire in prisms!

There was a kiss! as awed Chrysóstom knew:
"One lallapalousa of a smackeroo,"
He marveled (in Greek of Byzantium).

Space and time
Rang with a wild vibration, riot of rhyme.
All heaven was riled and rarin'.
Is so yet,
Judging by hints antennae, spectra get
To sass at astronomers: from each nebula hums
A mischievous heat
sets dancing all their sums.

POSTCARD FROM MINNESOTA

Last night I scrawled on a postcard *Love and Kisses*
In their curlicues: runes and doodles.
Now I ruminate: *kiss*. What it meant?
Self's mirror image? A mercury world we're a-glitter in?
Or maybe like sharing a world?
Another dimension:
     beyondness?
         Beyond the great fourth
— Speed-of-light razzle-dazzle in space —
There's a fifth one? The heart's
Gravitational stress on event?

  Here watching for dawn by a lake in Minnesota
  On a deck
  Of the barn-red lodge, at the hour it's delicious
    shivering:
  All of the east expectant
        — holding —
            gorgeous,
  Like curtains hung for a jubilee of sultans.
  The many-a-mile-wide water waits, all nods, a
  Decal of the airy hues there — hues, not colors — ,
  Decal of their silk on graininess of sailcloth.
  The long lake-levels
  Pull southward, crinkling a little, as if on rollers.
  Over the frosty glitter
  Some diving ducks, offshore, rump-up go under;
  Some Canada geese, wings pumping, beaks directional,
  Are skimming the wild-rice patch, the blowing
    lake-grass.

  Above, just over the jigsaw ridge of jack pine
  The heron, its black

Pick javelin-sharp, its black wings jagged as hemlock,
Black shin-rack hanging,
Flaps out of Jurassic canyons to this morning.

What a kiss is for, I was wondering. All's a part of it.
The dawn wind over the fin-rich water's part of it.

Wind cool, wind husky with skunk — over fern,
    through cedar —
On the lake does a dusky shuffle now. Like echoes
Of the loon, last night, on the full moon's zigzag
    catwalk.

And here, by the open porch-rail,
With a bowl of the old-rose raspberries, nestled
    yesterday
In your blue bandanna
        (Hard-lacquered
        Blackberries you plunk in a pail, but these you
        nestle),
                just yesterday, after the downpour,
Sun scorching our skin, leaves chill, with a rinse of
    raindrops.

Wild berries. Their flesh a honeycomb, hexagonal,
Curled in on themselves like the universe,
    outside-inside.
A Moebius trick — we can taste it.
Now a-bob on a level of cream, as embossed on vellum.
I glaze them in gilt with a swirl of our buckwheat honey
Trailed from a spoon,
Then sway it to spell out *love*
In script like the dawn's own gold on the medieval
Initial O of the bowl, its rose and ivory
— With a fine enough line you twirl *e* before *l* goes
    under.

But to bobble them, half afloat!

                               and to topple them over

The spoon-rim (its cozy oval

Drawn snug in the lips' twin curve), to fumble them

Up, and to mull on the tongue

                         those chummy, tumbling —

Inside them, a tickle of honey the tongue-tip thrills on —

And to crush, crush up lusher the pulp, red cells a fission

Of tiny electrical tingles,

A chain reaction — synaptic, galactic — no difference —

And to feel how they tease, a seed in the teeth, wedged
    testy,

Just a hint of cantankerous earth, old rancor's relish — !

                "... a world in a grain of sand ..."

And to sense, in the flesh of things, in their flow, a
    beyondness,

Power poured as from outer space — !

The kiss:

I suppose it meant something like this?

Like sharing a world?

                Not everyone's maybe.

                      Yours ...

PLATO: THE KISS

Τὴν ψυχήν, Ἀγάθωνα φιλῶν, ἐπὶ χείλεσιν ἔσχον·
ἦλθε γὰρ ἡ τλήμων ὡς διαβησομένη.

Plato (*Anthology*, V, 78)

That was my very soul that stole to the lips in our kissing.

Thinking to pass — poor thing! — over from me into you.

A SONG OF THE POET H'I HSI

Palms cool, like rain her ways, the Lady Yin.
Not so her sudden lord and love, who sprang
Spang from his desert noon. The chimes begin

When these two meet, from lands afar. His skin,
If kissed, a thrill of salt, hot sandy tang.
Toes curled in rainy moss, the Lady Yin.

Green lotus, twilight pool — a nixie grin
As naked girls flick silver? Planets hang,
Wink their gold desert eyelid. Chimes begin.

Bed curtains wink their chinky rings. Her chin
Alongside his till lips meet. Then rings rang!
"Ô pluies!" — the cool rings' raillery — "Aidez Yin!"

The kiss, though! circles curling, and within,
Half-circles curling tongue-tips. Sweet shebang!
Sweet yen, for green eye, gold eye. Chimes begin

When, kissing, they enfold, are rolled — unspin
Each where the other first lay. The Lord Yang,
Like ferny earth at evening. Lady Yin,
Flushed desert rose, lash salty. Chimes begin.

DAWN SONG

. . . to flute the pneuma . . .

Dearest, sleep. Bright night is gone.
Sleep away the dark of dawn.
    It's cold water now for drinking,
    Lids in the cold mirror blinking:

Face of clay, old trashy head.
Dearest, what of what you said?
    Such a one as this before me —
    Such, the midnight kisses swore me?

You said I was — thus and so.
You said — a bit more, you know.
    Mostly, high baroque was spoken;
    Mirror — chill of wind chimes — broken.

Never ivy twined so tight,
Held sprung alabaster right.
    Never, so in ivy sighing,
    At a stand were birth and dying.

Once another, great books say,
Made me out of the cold clay;
    Meant the dust I wear for glory —
    But of course, of course! *Our* story:

Lo, I lay cold clay alone
Till your hand sprung flesh and bone.
    Easter then: the world's untombing;
    Even lunar ash ablooming.

(Such entrusting, yours to me!
Hide your eye: the enchanted tree
    Twined with lightning Eve our mother!
    Such entrusting of each other!)

Love whose joy is second cause,
Cantilevering great laws
    On the porphyry corbel, knew you;
    Laughed to flute the pneuma through you:

"Body floral and velour,
Stir the dullard. Mull amour
    Of your honey, sun, or fertile
    Moon of melon, cotes of myrtle."

What he so projected, you
Took in hand, dear, and saw through.
    He in fangy strata laid me,
    Till you to his image made me.

Image: in the dismal sink,
Skinny, shivering, I blink.
    Back to the deep bed go weaving,
    Which — the glass or you? — believing?

Glass is glass. No inwit there
Stunned the emblazoned dove in air.
    What if shiny mirror shame it?
    All the darkness swore — acclaim it!

Though the flesh you crooned as sweet
Is sad matter on the street,
    Here's your loam for love and wonder:
    High perfume's a root far under.

In your nights of lightning bloom
Exhalations from the tomb.
  Odds say: stock of man's no bubble.
  So lay faith. But love lay double.

Double? One and one's our three:
I to you, love, you to me
  Were the two wings of one dove
  Radiant moon's the halo of.

Dearest, sleep. Bright night is gone.
Sleep away the dark of dawn.
  Stretch and yawn: your stir and murmur
  Root the entwining ivy firmer.

CARDIOLOGICAL

Ten heartbeats back our lips were touching. Ten?
Sixteen now, call it. Twenty-something. Truth
Can't manage this, can't get the hang of numbers.
Forty, and counting . . .

                        As the seas might drive,
Surge over surge, survivors from a raft
Their fingertips had touched once.

                             Stop that surge?
Stop, you can say to every clock but one
— Steeple-clock, travel-clock, cuckoo-clock — all but one:
The heart, with its red-jeweled steady movement, moves
This moment, this now, this all-our-life away,
Earth, with its birds and steeples, all away.

The prouder, the more impulsive, the more it takes.

Worse: our good moments, song, the mug swung high,
Gaze brimming gaze, the very clod upsoaring,
Joy at its most convulsive — even in dream —
Sting, like a lash, the stumbling heart — stampeding
With *more! yet more!* its irreversible beat.

TIDE TURNING

Through salt marsh, grassy channel where the shark's
A rumor — lean, alongside — rides our boat;
Four of us off with picnic-things and wine.
Past tufty clutters of the mud called *pluff*,
Sun on the ocean tingles like a kiss.
About the fourth hour of the falling tide.

The six-hour-falling, six-hour-rising tide
Turns heron-haunts to alleys for the shark.
Tide-waters kiss and loosen; loosen, kiss.
Black-hooded terns blurt kazoo-talk — our boat
Now in midchannel and now rounding pluff.
Lolling, we eye the mud-tufts. Eye the wine.

The Atlantic, off there, dazzles. Who said wine-
Dark sea? Not this sea. Not at noon. The tide
Runs gold as chablis over sumps of pluff.
Too shallow here for lurkings of the shark,
His nose-cone, grin unsmiling. *Cr-ush!* the boat
Shocks, shudders — grounded. An abrupt tough kiss.

Our outboard's dug a mud-trough. Call that *kiss?*
Bronze knee bruised. A fair ankle gashed. With "wine-
Dark blood" a bard's on target here. The boat
Swivels, propeller in a pit, as tide
Withdraws in puddles round us — shows the shark-
Grey fin, grey flank, grey broadening humps of pluff.

Fingers that trailed in water, fume in pluff.
Wrist-deep, they learn how octopuses kiss.
Then — shark fins? No. Three dolphins there — *shhh!* — arc
Coquettish. As on TV. Cup of wine

To you, slaphappy sidekicks! with the tide's
Last hour a mudflat draining round the boat.

The hourglass turns. Look, tricklings toward the boat.
The first hour, poky, picks away at pluff.
The second, though, swirls currents. Then the tide's
Third, fourth — abundance! the great ocean's kiss.
The last two slacken. So? We're free, for wine
And gaudier mathematics. Toast the shark,

Good shark, a no-show. Glory floats our boat.
We, with the wine remaining — done with pluff —
Carouse on the affluent kisses of the tide.

STAFF MEETING,
ASTRONOMY DEPARTMENT

Reveling summer left   her flesh its tawny bloom,
mane of meadows, scent   heady in a room
where committees twiddle —   he acclaimed her sun,

being but dumb earth,   lank penumbral one
any sun endangers   (in wild heaven born);
he swung, axis veering,   out of orbit torn.

Amethyst: dim planets   potter off apart.
Uncontrollable heaven   antiquates our chart;
old professor's pointer   chatters where it taps:
frontiers burst on earth, but   — on celestial maps?

Yes, new sun in heaven;   yes, new eyes to see.
Teacher, after Einstein   who's for Ptolemy?

Still the brooding schoolmen,   chin in fingers' cup —
shake your mane, wild heaven;   shake those schoolmen up.

A SCHOLAR WONDERS

Their human love — confusing! Off they fling
Flurry of skirt, shirt — heavens, everything!
And then, heaped dense and shining, mostly prize
The long long gazing in each other's eyes.

NEWS FROM PROVENCE

Irai per tot achaptan
De chascuna un bel semblan
Per far domna soiseubuda
Tro vos me siatz renduda . . .

Bertran de Born

Now Pound in his omnium-gatherum, rags and riches,
Tells how to make a lady — I mean construct her —
And here's how you do it — pencils out! He snitches
Key parts from the lot — shin here, shank there —
    even plucked her
A tummy with all appurtenance. Spotting which is
A body's best, ol' Ez the Ripper shucked her,
Cross-stitching (our Frankenstein) a patchwork Siren,
The "imagined lady" some hanker for — say Byron

Who jaunted about a-basting up his idol
From snatches of girl. And boy. And a swatch of sister.
These made-up loves have many a plus. Denied, 'll
Not scratch or scream. Abused, won't chafe or blister.
Last longer. Are scuff-resistant (time and tide'll
Plumb ruin the rest). Won't pretty-pout, *You missed her?*
True, they're a freak if seen. One wonders, "Who the
Deuce have we here?" A *domna soiseubuda.*

That's Provençal, where Pound was cabined, cribbing.
Imagined lady, we'd say, in God's good English.
English? You want a rhyme on that, ad-libbing?
Rhyme-schemes from the foreign bards are much too jinglish.
Ours? Loose as a lonelies' bar, where all sip fibbing,
Where single and not so single pass for singlish.
Italian rhymes, they involve you, like spaghetti
— A word which, here in the midland, rhymes with *steady.*

But steady is what our singles aren't. See *those* two?
Last night they were halves of *these* two, swapping blisses
Like pennies matched. (*Ottava rima's* s'pos' to
Mosy.) *Imagined ladies.* Imagined kisses
The theme of our meditation, though drawing close to
A melancholy sounding of love's abysses.
The moral — so perk your ears up, sons and daughters —:
Don't dabble in raspberries by the morning waters

Unless you're the pure of heart. Or they'll debauch you.
You start with, "The tongue fits nifty in! Dee-licious!"
Then: "Tickly! Like lips the summer chapped." They've
    caught you!
Next you think, "The convenience too!" Oh vicious!
You oughtn't to dawdle with aught so naughty, ought you?
Better let Horror bellow, "Bosh!" Suspicious
How many who'd snicker reading "lips like cherries"
Guzzle, come kissing time, like cubs in berries.

Let stern Decorum trumpet out: "Them rasses-
Berries is not no kiss! Them fruits is menaces!"
It's simulacra you're after? Common as grass is.
You'll find as many canals to pole as Venice's.
Everywhere nature mimics lad's and lass's.
Art likewise. You can inflate — like God in *Genesis*
A-breathing a soul in — life-size dollies, rubber.
Disposable. Leave no skeletons. Chummy blubber.

Yours to adore in your way. Yours to slubber.

SONNET ALMOST PETRARCHAN

*And there was that row with the German-Burgundian
female . . .*

Canto IX

He stared — lean tusk of a man — and dreamed each breast a
Moon-cameo sheer in silk, her maize hair swaying
Over them as she danced, a glamour playing
In the cool eye that swept his own. *His* fiesta!
He, Sigismondo Pandolfo Malatesta!
Who prettied the church! And she care? Out sashaying!

He splintered the door that night, where those were staying,
Stabbed her young man. Hands, hauling, half undressed a
Glow like the stormy moon's.

               What, writhe and dare
Breathe deeper to flash effrontery?

               Flushed, he sunk
— Once, twice — his blade in her shining life. Maize hair
Gagging a cry, she stumbled and —

               like one drunk
He hunkered: each grunt that frothed in her blood, each hiss
Of animal rapture scavenging: *Kiss! Kiss!*

THE YEAR, 1520

... in the country, not far from Calais ...

As one who — and so we're a-sonneting? — one who
Sleeps with a casual beauty in the brush:
At morning yawns, amused and tender, "You?
Who are you, stranger?" And the kisses rush.
His finger, reverent, broods on brow, on nose
Tipped with its dust of gold, on flutter of lash.
He jokes at her comb, "A princess?" smoothing clothes
Richer than sundown showed —

                     on a sudden, a flash
Of armor in all the fields around, a thunder
Of oriflammes smarting of smoke and towns afire;
Men-at-arms with hot coals for eyes; and under
Banners, her throne; her ape, her fool and friar.
Hoarse helmets buzzing obeisance raise the girl,
Who sweeps from her cheek, eye blazing, earth and a curl —

PLAZA DE TOROS

Madrid. A las cinco . . .

As — for how else do poems go? — as some
Torero in his bravery, gold and red,
Ignites with a playing wrist that ton of plumb
Thunder, all testy rump, hot hovering head —

Toes so, set like a wager, risk a thigh
Bright in its cocky silk, with nerve and bone;
Lids lowered see the terrible horn go by,
And still he rolls like a flag in battle, blown
Crisscrossing —

        Turns a languorous shoulder then
Full on that savage bafflement, in throes.
A rapture of handkerchiefs. Tiptoe, girls and men
Wave till the crowd's in flower, a snowy rose.
Blood on the dust, dark blood on wrist and knee.
"As, you began —?"
        And glory on: as *he.*

A KISS FROM HER

Εὐρώπης τὸ φίλημα, καὶ ἢν ἄχρι χείλεος ἔλθῃ,
ἡδύ γε, κἂν ψαύσῃ μοῦνον ἄκρου στόματος·
ψαύει δ' οὐκ ἄκροις τοῖς χείλεσιν, ἀλλ' ἐρίσασα
τὸ στόμα τὴν ψυχὴν ἐξ ὀνύχων ἀνάγει.

Rufinus (*Anthology*, V, 14)

A kiss from her! Her mouth, coming even close to your own,
   how
Sweet! How sweet if it brush ever so lightly the lip.
But that's not her kind of kiss. No: drawing your mouth
   close, closer,
   She drinks of your soul; it flows — currents from finger
   and toe.

ADVICE FROM THE CLASSICS

Catullus, v

So let's live — really *live!* — for love and loving,
honey. Guff of the grumpy old *harrumph*ers,
what's it worth? Is it even worth a penny?
Suns go under, to soar again in glory
— *they* can. Smothered, our little light, we're done: one
unarousable dead of night forever.
Now's our time for commodity of kisses!
Hundreds! thousands! and hundreds of them! thousands!
More! galore! And a dividend! A bonus!
So. Then post, sitting pretty on our millions,
sums that none — we the least — make head or tail of.
Don't let's know, even us. Or evil eyes might
glitter green, over such a spell of kisses.

SLAPSTICK I

Meditation for the Morning: Linguistics and the Kiss

. . . illo purpureo ore suaviata . . .
         Catullus, xlv

Love and Kisses we write, on the backs of our Tru-Kolor
    Fotos.
Now I think about *kiss*.
Ugly word in the mouth, with its—ouch!—little dental-pick *k;*
Its vowel with no music at all, and that snake-hiss of *s*'s.

And the cock-a-snook rhymes it comes schlepping. But
    better not think.
Kiss is cousin to *cuss*, a good word: *cuss* can cuss, but *kiss*
    kiss?
Not a word the lips linger on lovingly,
Although meant to mean: lingering lips.

Φίλημα's a lovemaking word now: your own, Aphrodite.
You can throw yourself too, *con amore* and how, into *bacio*.
Young Catullus imported that word,
Put the kibosh on *osculum*
Bringing *basium* down from Verona — known later for lovers.

Basium — that's from *sua* [*v/b*]*ium* (sweet):
Suabium inside out, as the lips wish to be in a kiss.

There's that word again — *kiss!*
Northern Puritans spat that flat *kiss*.

27

Couldn't open their mouths in the cold?
So no full-mouth affection?

Well, we're stuck with the word.
                              How get rid of it?
                                   How kiss it off?

WITH A BLONDE IN A BAR-BOOTH

While you decide, a cigarette for poise?
Your breath inspires it, and your breath destroys.

"Meaning by that?"

                         I only said: Your breath,
The same that gives it glory, gives it death.

"Wait, light me, love. And so —?"

                              What all things say:
Only, how very dark's the end of day.

"Cozy though, here."

                    Inhale! The living spark
Glows till your lip's a lotus in the dark;
Floats you, a rose-gold lotus. Cheeks indrawn.

Well, we're a catch of breath, love. Caught and gone.

DESIGN: A FURTHER WORD

. . . If design govern . . .

Dull gold of oak leaves falling where they might:
A patch of Byzantium in the undergrowth
For the trillium, white arms dancing —

                                But, like an oath
Half hissed in a quiet chapel,
                    this
                this sight:
One flower had pierced one leaf, torn it not quite
Apart as the poignant arms would lift. A troth
Dismaying to flower and leaf: one doom for both.
You've heard of a crown of thorns, of a Persian rite
Impaling its victim — stark — in heaven's own light?

Place, time, and weather combined so here:
                               a-sprawl
On its gibbet inches up, the oak leaf, tight
Spikes into flesh, tormented his blonde upright
Tormenter. A whim of the wind? Or rain's soft fall
Adduced — of the earth's own virtue — vice and awl?

A BALLAD OF KISSES AND COMBS

When you were a little child, my love,
Silk hair long as you,
Mother gave you a comb and a kiss,
Drew you close as she combed "like this" —
But you ripened out of her arms to his,
Tighter arms than true.

Made a stranger welcome, love,
But he was ill-come there.
You had a kitten teased the fire,
Flowering-snow and a rose in briar —
Played them all on a shy desire,
And the rant of his night-long hair.

Walk away unlucky, love;
Possess the wind and rain.
You had a home, an oaken home,
But his who came was rove and roam —
Much he'd care for the broken comb
Where the bed-length tresses lay.

Walk along the water, love,
Where the salt sea hurls its wave;
Where the woods weave rose in the gold to die,
And dawn from her tumbled dress steps high —
Meadow, easy knee to the sky,
And the blind, deep-kissing grave.

DAUGHTER, AGE 4

Came traipsing to my bed today:
    No other gave so much
Rough-and-tumble tenderness,
    Was such a flower to touch.

Girl of the morning, rowdy rose,
    My own as none was mine
Of those serene and witty ones,
    The tall languorous line,

What's to wish you? (Who's the girl
    Heard any such word said?)
May you, the shapely years at hand,
    Vex such another bed.

FIRST DATE

Be careful whom you kiss. You never know.
Men wade Niagara, upstream, the white flow
Shearing from ankle, shinbone
                — but
                  slow . . . slow . . .

SALLY AND ALISON: JULIE. AND JOAN.

Each
so alive with
wind at skirt or curl,
turned, a nice rhyming,
every last girl,
girl of every season
in the changing park,
each? On a date with
marble and the dark?

Vague and
blue April —
love a touchy thing!
Summer: rough sunflowers
scuffle where they cling.
Autumn: fern lash on
cheek a
wild-honey glow —

January, what of her?
Dim, in the dim snow.

April,
if you kiss, no
bird in bush or hand.
August, salt lips that
scour like sea-sand.
Autumn: grain swaying in
arms that gather
rich
and slow —

January, what of her?
Blind, in the blind snow.

Take to bed
April,
and clown away despair.
Summer: such surfing in
play of seaweed hair!
Autumn: at dawn all
offered, soul aglow,
eyes' amber dance, fern
curling, head to toe —

January? That girl — ?
In the lost snow.

April lovers,
hush them
with a lark in view.
August, by a raw cove
where the coots halloo.
Autumn of the
slow gold
where the hazel shucks are thick,
poppy lips parted
by a bristled
rick —

Crisp: the world turning
whets an edgy air.
Breath of frost? Soon . . .
somewhere
off
there.

These knees,
October,
these to blanch and go —
she,
our warm breather,
wade the waste snow?
Not a shrub? Nowhere,
love, to lie
low?

Girl
of every season
in the changing park,
each
on a date with
marble and the dark?
Each
so alive with
wind at skirt or curl,
turned, a nice rhyming,
every
last
girl
?

THE MADNESS IN VERMONT THIS FALL

Stripped of its summer wealth,
Can the bough be wan as a root?
Go dingy in spells of frost,
Untrimmed of its bird, its fruit?

No — trees go wild at the thought.
They know what they mean to do.
Wild trees, gone out of your head?
Do you burn to go south, you too?

Are you trying to be fruit, is it that?
Banana, wild cherry, or plum,
Lemon or apricot, grape
Glow of burgundy's from?

Worse, are you envying birds?
Playing oriole, tanager — such?
Long to be tropical wings?
Wildfire in the trees, too much!

Can we keep our heads in a world
With its yankee wit so lost
That the woods are a cry for fire,
And minding the fire is frost?

LOVE IN THE WESTERN WORLD

Love in the autumn, then. We love beneath the
    Foliage of the summer groves afire.
        Rafter and lath infested —
            The live wire.
No news in this: what eyes have met and rested
    In any weather but the signs were dire?

Those in the painted cave, who shrugged at rumor
    Of kin with a bigger rockpile and The Sling
        — He to emboss the bison,
            She to sing.
Or at bay on the walls of Rome, the night horizon
    Lurid with campfires in a hissing ring.

Or Deerfield. Yule and moonlight. While dementia
    Howls in the wood for tomahawk debris.
        Gloucester, the wintry shipping,
            Fire at sea.
Or in our time any corner, sirens ripping
    Into the living flesh. But he and she

Deep in themselves, mellifluous. Eyes together
    Open such vistas in the autumn scene
        It lopes away, grey peril;
            And, between,
The falling leaves, reversing, lift and carol
    Back to the nodding suavities of green:

And all's the original garden where that Adam
  Dotes on the girl there, curled in flowery sleep.
    Angels though — baroque shoulder,
      Cheek scarred deep?
So dead a West? Not a Nova now? they smoulder;
  Even Ram, Bear, Bull, heaven's mavericks: croupy sheep?

HOW TO TELL THE GIRLS FROM THE FLOWERS

Both sway. Are fragrant mostly. Wells for dew.
Have their one season early. Tell the two
First by their gaze, half hid with lash or leaf:
Eyes of the girl go deeper. Wells for grief.

PIERRE DE RONSARD,
LES AMOURS DE MARIE, *XIX*

Marie, levez-vous, ma jeune paresseuse!
Jà la gaie alouette au ciel a fredonné,
Et jà le rossignol doucement jargonné,
Dessus l'épine assis, sa complainte amoureuse.
Sus, debout! allons voir l'herbelette perleuse,
Et votre beau rosier de boutons couronné
Et vos œillets mignons auxquels aviez donné
Hier au soir de l'eau d'une main si soigneuse.
Harsoir en vous couchant vous jurâtes vos yeux
D'être plus tôt que moi ce matin éveillée;
Mais le dormir de l'aube aux filles gracieux
Vous tient d'un doux sommeil encor les yeux sillée.
Çà, çà! que je les baise et votre beau tétin
Cent fois, pour vous apprendre à vous lever matin.

TIME TO BE UP, MARIE

Time to be up, Marie, young sleepyhead!
The meadowlark's already in the sky;
The nightingale that keeps her thorny bed
Already's sung and hushed the lovelorn cry.
Let's revel now in grassiness and dew
And hail your rosebush with its corals crowned;
Your clove pinks too — I watched, last evening, you
Water with loving hand the garden 'round.
Last night, on going to bed, Lord! Lord! you swore
That you'd be up and doing, the first to rise.
Yet slumber on at dawn? Sink more and more
In morning-sleep girls love? A kiss for eyes;
For breasts, here, there a kiss. Some hundred strewing,
I'll teach you, dreamer, to be up and doing.

LOVE AMONG THE PHILOSOPHERS

And so whan they were a-bedde both, Sir Trystram
rememberde hym of his fyrst love, La Belle Isoude, and
suddeynly he was all dismayde, and other chere made he none
but with clyppinge and kyssinge. As for other fleyshely
lustys, Sir Trystram had never ado with her: such mencion
makyth the ffreynshe booke.

You, moody miss who wanted more, recall
Stair stumbled, key sought, fluster in the hall,
Kisses on kisses glistering, and that's all?

Half-heart or whole, we've heart for kissing. True.
Who needs a ffreynshe booke parleying of ado?
It's kissing done, knights-errant pull askew.

When the impetuous soul elects to stray,
The flesh turn sudden saint, and have its day?
Interpret fundamentally *feet* of clay?

Let's speculate — that's our verb now. Fix a drink,
Your hair a mournful oriflamme at the sink.
If links of reason give, why gin's a link.

The soul has claques palavering it's no beast
— Yet roll on the floor so often, at love's feast?
Well, there's the flesh to keep it straight, at least

This virtuous night. No purlieus here to skulk,
Fidelity stalwart in its stubby hulk.
(Not charmed by my *sic* and *ergo*, dear? Must sulk?)

Anatomize *kiss*. Since kissing Judas came
And kissed that kiss of his, they ring the same?
Cold couples kiss and kiss, in Judas' name.

40

Whereas: that other fleyshely lust, so called,
Longs for a firm affection. Sinks appalled
Seeing itself a stand-in. Though blackballed,

Glum lovely, count your blessings. Science gives
Ghostly advice on chumming with negatives.
(The very stuff we're of, it's water in sieves.)

And: here's a thought rings jubilant in the gloom:
Souls on their own, what noble capers bloom
Seeing old fussy bluenose in the tomb.

As for that vaunted heaven harridans bless,
Crusaders storm, nuns skimp for, who'd take less
Than even dreams of the common couch confess?

Such meditations dazzle: bliss too bright.
Dear, what a shapely yawn. Going early? Right.
Only let's kiss, who never dreamed good night.

SLAPSTICK II

Meditation for the Morning:
On This Matter of Instrumentality

Now I think about *kiss*.
What it means? — but avoid definition.
"Conjunctified mugs with flip-flopping of labial blab-flaps."
So Webster defines it? A facy flapdoodle is all?
It's one of those poor *pis-allers*
The soul must put up with to humor
Its tie to the *rerum natura*, this doo-funny world.
All atoms, subatoms, assembly of Tinkertoy parts.

Take the body's weird gear meant to manifest Tender Emotion.

Human instrumentality, *ick!*

Zum Beispiel, in Orchestra Hall.

See that stage with its — *awk!* — wacky knackery.
Bosh as in Bosch!
What a hockshop of chock-a-block schlock!
Chin-fiddles, shin-fiddles,
Catgut racked over — whatzisses? — thingummies warped in
   the rain?
And the bed-springs there, twisty as junk,
Upended to twitch and to twitter, go *twing* and go *twang*.
Tinny tubes that slurp slipslop in tubby tubes
— Under the sink!
And — *ook!* — bullfroggy burping spittoons.
Then that wryneck old three-legged hunchback,
His ear-to-ear smirk at the sky!

From these foo-foos and druck,
      fiddle-faddle, flimflam,
           the Ninth Symphony soars?

    You're damn tootin' it soars!
      Bet your boots!

So, Maestro,
The podium, please.

Then the souls are on high! In True Beautiful shapes
(All the mouldy old mush-words in vigor again!),
Souls a-soar, fresh and luminous too, as they'll float
Over boneyards that Fabulous Day
When the skeletons scuttle
          skedaddle in scads
             to the sky.

So it goes.
    So our heart goes *ka-boom* and *ka-boom*.
     So our lungs go *ka-whish* and *ka-whoosh*.
So our music is made.
    So we . . .
      kiss.

A SUMMER LOVE

Flourish, with black-raspberry cone

All of us lovers! when the summer sun
pales to the south, and tidy fall's begun,
troop to our rakes and bonfires — off we go,
leaving the gull his bitter kingdom. So:

a keepsake on departure? Of what kind?
What can we give, what something none could find
— no doting husband or fond fussing wife
uncover in some bureau? Found, a knife
(sure as that shoddy rhyme) to either's heart,
the trusting man or woman's. So we part,
no gift but this: bare fistful, purplish, pearled.
Our melting present in a melting world.
Friend of the cool and shady, shy of sun;
kissed away quick by tonguing, quick to run.
Flushed without fervor; without firmness, blunt.
Not to be held — so slipslop — to account.
A thing not meant to last. Nor get us far.

Call it a sort of rhyme for what we are.

SPLEEN

Catullus, lxx

Well, Catullus. So you knew.
Raged: *what these women coo*

to their lovers, write in air;
find a sea, and write there.

Once I had a girl burned
in my ear words she learned

maybe in a book, or heard
on the loose street slurred.

Tried to write it — one stroke
saw the page curl in smoke.

Wrote it on the air instead:
singing birds fell down dead.

Wrote it on the running wave:
saw the sea fishes' grave.

Roman, here's a better way:
words the pretty lips say,

cut them in your white thigh
for a thought to have by;

gouge a scar fingers find
when the long nights grind;

where, though sweaty limbs thresh,
grief and shame are proud flesh.

A WINTER LOVE ONCE LONG AGO

For hours and hours and hours he leaned
his fever on the glass;
saw through ice the frozen street,
the frozen autos pass;

but never saw the car that once
came docile to his door.
Stared, till beneath the winter moon
no passers anymore.

At midnight, three, and four o'clock,
demented streets of ice.
He heard his heart lurch barely once
where love would lift it twice,

and mock with: "Glass and emptiness.
The one you love is such.
What's left but cautery of snow
for lips that burned too much?

"Go drag your shanks bare-naked on
December's frozen mold.
The body of the one you love
is many times as cold."

Or so it said. And yet, and yet —
that window and that street!
No bed of clover, bed of straw
— in all the years! — so sweet.

BACK TO BASICS

1.

Contribution to the Heart Fund

. . . ka-boom, ka-boom . . .

Please fill 'er up and better check the oil.
Add cup of water slowly. Bring to boil.
Deposit fifty cents for overtime.
New! For Your Wash-Day Pleasure! Gobbles Grime!
Cheeseburger special and a glass of beer.
The men to fix the whoozy-whats are here.

"Cut the iambics, hey! *Duh-dumm, duh-dumming!*
Stick to American rhythm. Real! — like plumbing.
Flush and it flows, authentic. Don't *duh-dee* it!"

Heard your own heartbeat lately? Want to "free" it?

2.

Bite

Rhyme's where the bite is. Tough rhyme. Not *quest-lest.*
For Li Po in his east, for Trakl west,
Mandelstam northward and Machado south,
Verse without rhyming was a toothless mouth.

3.

A Defense of the Method

Hey love! hey love! Let's take a break, midkiss.
I've had a notion here I'd like to hiss
At dumb-dumbs huffy that our lips can rhyme
A B A B. Like so, dear. Keeping time.
Do B again! Hey great! Now do the A.
Aren't we the ones for prosody, you say?

Know what the schoolgirls taught me after school?
Either the lips meet rhyming
                                    or they drool.

RHYME ROYAL

I'm typing. There's a tangle. Two keys kiss.
Kissing, they make a poem-thing. Like this:

With *you,* life flows *assuring.* Losing *u,*
        It shrinks to *ass ring* — ring of asses! True.

There's augury in our bungles, Doktor, hey?
News from Vienna? Shamans, clack away.

THE ORIGIN OF MYTH

For Daphne, decorating the tree

Christmas again. And the kings. And the camels that
   Travel like shanties collapsing. We hurl
      Fistfuls of shivery bliss in the night on a
         Tree like some luminous ghost of a girl.

Men had a myth: how Apollo (no kin of mine)
   Flushing in shrubs a bent shoulder and head,
      Snorted and plunged for her, lofty blood thundering —
         "Oh," she said. "*Oh!*" she said. There's a girl sped.

Hovered high hurdles; flashed a fine knee or so,
   Flashed a fine — Ovid says, how her flounce flew.
      Cornered, she crinkled to armfuls of laurel, her
         Heartbeat in bark ebbing. Likely: I knew

Much the same story: once scuffled fall foliage;
   Caught the soft runaway, crushed to my brow
      Curls that turned holly leaves, pin-pointy, hissing things;
         Felt the warm bark alive. Heaven knows how

These had gone walking all the broad autumn,
   Poked in gold cubbyholes down the dark run;
      Fumbled in foliage crisp as old tinsel, and
         Tussled and scuffed too much. Blurting: "Been fun."

Fun? — but it wasn't fun. Blundered half purposely
   Into each other — through wool such delight?
      "I want you all," he choked, "cornflower, corn-tassel!"
         "Oh," she laughed, redder then. "*Oh!*" she wept,
            white.

"Snug rough and tumble here? Fun in a furrow bunk?
    What would you do, gamin? Turn to a tree?"
        "I don't know." Tears flickered. "I don't know." Hems
            flinging.
            Whitely defiant though, "Try. And you'll see."

Down the dense calendar's black and red stubble field
    Gone, the October girl. Plunging, he kept
        Eyes on a — cypress? Dead mistletoe? Myrtle-bush?
            Oak that would crash on him? Willow that wept?

Ashen as sassafras? Judas-tree? Juniper?
    Trekking November, he scuffed the dull days.
        Caught her at Christmas, in cedar gloom wassailing.
            Somber, and swirling dark rum as she sways:

"What's a gone girl to you? Better: forever-things.
    All the fall-forest bit; all the dense kiss.
        'Turn to a tree?' " Taking tinsel and bangles, she
            Pinned, in her ponytail, tree-glitter. "This

Crimson for lips, the fall foliage ranting;
    Gold, for that foliage blurred the wind's bliss;
        Blue, for cool gloom in the cornstubble starlight;
            Silver, for lashes lay salt to the kiss.

"Bittersweet, mistletoe gussy my goldilocks."
    Arms like boughs bending, she downed the dark rum.
        "Summer love — tumbleweed! Winter's your evergreen,
            Stars in her hair when the camel-trains come."

KISMET

Here's a happenstance — you'll hear it? —
though it's wickedly romantic.
Could be, not a soul alive that
gives a hoot for Once-Upon-A . . .

Once upon a time, however,
Lord of Luristan, Thelorak,
kissed a mighty kiss of kisses.
West of Babylon it happened,
south of Kirman Shah, by Shiraz.

Nomad from the North, Thelorak,
feared in Ku Galu and Shushtar,
feared in Luristan: his armies
hovered like the sign for thunder.

Luristan, that made the bronzes:
charm, for shooing witch from pony,
helmet, for the eyes to glow in,
chain mail, casing boy as beetle.

But in all that land of clangor,
none so bronze as he, Thelorak.
Bronze, the scowling brow of helmet,
bronze, the scowling brow beneath it;
couldn't tell where cheek met cheekpiece;
couldn't tell the one fist, naked,
from that other fist, in gauntlet.
Shuck his body-armor off, and
there's a man of bronze beneath it.

See that face: as gashed with acid,
like the war god's own, in temples.

That's his love, the war god. Other
love he mocks as pig-sty pother.

On that day: a surf of warriors
churns around Thelorak jaunting,
jounced about on choppy cruppers
over cobblestones in Kush Lo.
Holiest of cities, Kush Lo,
where the war god's temple threatened,
columns baring tusks, above them
cornice like a boar-snout curling.

There Thelorak came, steed rearing;
there he dared the darkened gullet,
flung like knives his glances 'round him.
Under gloom of porch, those glances
glitter on a couple kissing.
Deaf to all, that pair, the fellow
pasted to his she, she leaning
back on stone, a pallor rippling
— think of little waves in moonlight.

Slits of eye like slits of helmet,
hoarse Thelorak stared, cheek flaring,
saw the god of war besmirched where
lips were swabbing lips — their lapping
minding him of hogs in offal.
"Shove," he shouted, "shoats apart there!"
Chutes from saddlebow and stirrup,
tears the pair in two — ha! — hurls them:
her against the stonework, him half
scrambling under hooves of horses.

Her! He'd measure her, each feature:
widened eye and lips that widen,
widen not in love — in terror,

are about to scream. He stops them,
plugs a heel of hand across, but
head against the grime behind, she
tries to writhe away; on stone her
curls, a rustled cornsilk, crinkle,
spread — like grated spice — a fragrance.
Eyes beneath their floral fringes,
lilac — temple pools at evening
show so in a dusk of starlight.

Felt her lip against his calloused
palm — that lord — a-tremble, like some
newborn mite of life, a nestling.
With a thrust, his palm unstopped her
mouth, the lip drained pale, one corner
vivid with a fleck of crimson,
as she bit to hold despair in,
breast against his bruising buckle.

"Swiller of men's lips," he mocked her.
"Mopper of wet snouts in temples!"
Words she didn't hear, she twisting
as to see, beyond her shoulder,
panic under hooves of horses.
"What's this lapping lips?" he lashed with.
From her not a sound; lips breathless
held his eye
     — an impulse —
        "Show me!
Do your kiss-thing once forever.
Kiss to end these kisses." Bristling,
face all growl and grit he took her,
rolled her lip in his lips, this way,
that way, outside, inside, out —
          but
sudden, as if struck, a strangeness.

Shivered — he, the warrior? — loosed their
mouths, drew back a breath, as puzzled,
mulling on her lips, her lashes.
Once again, but slow, as groping,
laid his earthen lip to earthen
hers

> O rich and fertile earth is!
> How it flowers! How clean the furrows
> where the glossy plow unfurls them;
> how, with corn and wheat for promise,
> it cajoles with nurse and nourish.
> Savored mother earth, the man did,
> learned the way of roots exploring
> toward a breathless dark, the haunts of . . .
>
> Came on springs that — chilly, thrilling —
> croon like flutes afar, a spell that
> wild things in their burrows stir to;
> croon through sod, rock, lava, gravel,
> swell to — flood of floods! demolish
> fences, farmhouse, castle — kingdoms.
>
> Came on roots that heave earth-waters
> up through thew of spruce, of moosewood;
> hoist them high as boughs go, sluice them
> in the life of leaves, in bird song,
> stir a windy surf in tree tops,
> surf a-bob with moon, sun, planets.
>
> Then — amazement! — earth was airy,
> drinking every breath of heaven:
> North, white apple-scent of snowflake;
> East, the salt marsh, sea mist, sea bird;
> South, blue noon, anana, mango;
> West, the redfinch, cedar, sunset.

All of this — the earth, air, water —
burst in flame, a blinding moment's
insight into . . . ? into . . . ? Back toward
fertile earth we go, its furrows.

So it was, that kiss of kisses.
Seconds long. The horses stamping.
Lord Thelorak stared within him,
clouded brow, with back of fist on
newfound lips. Then slowly drew his
broadsword, glint of bronze, regarded
all its length . . .
                What happened next?
                                Well,
here the story ends. We wonder.
Judgment's up to you, and you there.
Maybe — you suppose? — he killed her?

BAROQUE POEM IN DUBIOUS TASTE

Sag ich euch absurde Dinge,
Denkt, dass ich Abraxas bringe ...
                                        Goethe

Our theme is:
the shape a poem ought to have.

Ought? Like a kiss.

                        Which is — even children learn —
a round of shapes that work to one shape. One
most human shape.

Like lips half opening to breathe *yes* on *yes*,
urge *yes* in all the many ways they know,
wing-tipping this way, that way tipped a little,
      lip-shape on shape of lips . . .

      Upper curve: slender, notched precisely, cool
      as mind itself, intense almost as mind,
      almost a thought and sensitive as thought,
      it speaks for the mind above — lean loftier upper.
      When two such meet — lord, lord! — the meeting of
        minds.

      The lower, though: all feeling, full as fruit,
      proxy for the rich body there below,
      proxy for all that treasure, throat to toe.
      More givable lip, that lower; more to take
      in between lips. And *Take me* it says best.

Merge *body* and *mind,* they blur to *blind and moody*
too often. But not here.
No: soul's in the four lips' fourfold interplay,

cool on cool, warm on warm
— like rounding the compass-rose, no end of changes
that a round shape has room for.

There's more to tell?
Like tongue-tip tentative on the neat teeth
        in neat half-circles:
lake-pebbles smooth in sun;
        tongue teeming above, below, on outer, inner,
       affectionate tally, tingling, to attemper
eight half-rings in conjunction —
                  flashy astronomers
once made such very models of the universe,
made nests of the singing rings, called *armillary,*
or named for his witty lordship, Boyle and *Orrery.*
Museums love their glittering ingenuities,
models of —
         something other than they meant to be?

"A kiss is like *that*? You're really gross, you know it?"

     No, baroque.
Baroque, like the shapes that nature
fondles to odd excess in deep-sea gorges,
sunken cathedrals, topsy-turvy, crockets
gashed, as by lightning, in contortions of lava,
into basalt, all honeycombed, into the core of it.

"Baroque?"

      Or say grotesque
for what goes on in the grottoes, pearl and coral.
A strange Arabian tale. Our *Open sesame,*
revealing — who knows in advance? Who dare surmise it?

"Ask me, I still say gross. I say: ridiculous!"

A poem: most like a kiss. A play of shapes
that search, researching over the perfect shape
to stop the moment-in-time and stamp it: *This.*

The moment in Minnesota once, and others.

And after the search, a closing, a coming clean
and they're apart

          a-hover, as on a precipice

      — appended tremulous: delicate diamond strung
      like cobweb, maybe, featured in a fairy tale,
      or milkweed silk, afield at night, a filament
      the moonlight's a fine laser on, in leafage —

      a closing, a coming clean
with soft click — like a key that turns on treasure —
   soft,
      like a jewelbox closing,
              repoussé.

WATCHING THE PLANES
COME IN AT LA GUARDIA

Joan's kiss
     — it pancakes —
           a flat smack.

                            But Jeanne!
The delicate approach, slow tilt and lean.
All hovering danger and delight.
                As when
Home, over mountain, sea, and chancy weather,
Plane and its shadow
          thrill
             and touch together.

LOVE AND DEATH

And yet a kiss, like blubber, 'd blur and slip,
Without the assuring skull beneath the lip.

SUNRISE BY MAGRITTE

Stare far in the dark. Who'd guess the dark could hide
So broad a water and the haunts across it?
Lake-presence that aches like a pressure felt inside,
Felt but unseen — no glow from heaven to gloss it.
No wind — for the wind's a kind of light — to toss it.
Till — dawn in the offing — sky and water show,
As lo! at the first of words, sea drew below,

Sky drew above, and land was land. Now more
Than pulsing of many waters in the night
This tension of heaven pressuring the shore.
Primal desire — like eyes that widen, bright,
Converting fervor of soul to flecks of light.
All sky's an about-to-happen; such a glance
Have hovering lovers as their lips advance.

The East, an alive pulsation, rose and gold,
Stillness building like crescendo of drums.
Urgency mounts — unbearable! — cannot hold
— And the sun! in a burst of dazzlement! Or comes
Cloud-scuttled, a living coal. Once, flinty thumbs
Struck flashes that flickered on our hunkering clan.
With sparks in a cave, the parabolas began.

The parabolas! Only a parable for fact?
Fact but the ferns of fancy stratified?
You — you see the sun half up, his standard act.
I — I see his carmine mouth, from the further side
Of space and time, on the world's pale lip. His bride.
Shyly at first, lean upper lip outcurled,
Then brushing with lower lip the brightening world.

Two curvatures that crisscross, earth and sun,
Each stinging the other to halation of glory.
Lasting how long in heartbeats, where *begun's*
Beginning of *over*? And the sequel sorry?
Joy soars to a pitch. And then —? Another story.
These kiss to the limit of measurable desire?
Beyond the endurable bliss, mere blinding fire?

Well, dawn's a delirium of the spheres. Our vanity
Commends the parental orgy there. But think:
It sprang — our madness — from the coolest sanity.
Consult in a sooty glass that sun, and blink:
One perfect circle, drawn classroom-clear. No chink,
No bobble. This Giotto's *O*, this orb, this ought,
Convulse like the flesh responding to a thought?

STEWARDESS FALLS FROM PLANE

Unusual bird, unusual words for you?
Earth whistled, and you came. As all girls do.

LOVE SONG FOR OUTER SPACE

*. . . that saying of Swedenborg that the intercourse
of angels is a conflagration of the whole being . . .*

W. B. Yeats

If all that talk of heaven's true
    (Only the grosser whimsy shed:
Cherubs a-larrupin' the lyre,
    Rumps roly-poly overhead),
If glory of consciousness return
    Like morning on the muddled blood,
If we are we, the same we yet,
    And stand together, as we stood,
And take such fire from each, as once
    Set gables of the town ablaze,
Made sootiest dark a dazzle, where
    Fire in the fire we blundered, dazed —
If so —? Blunt stubble of the flesh
    Enkindled beyond power to bear
Ruined us once — and if the soul's
    So combustible essence flare?

Often we had, come dull of dawn,
    Nothing to blend but tepid breath.
Once short of that, we've still in store
    Thrust of the long-careering death.
And: if the heavy flesh could soar
    Of its own weight a handbreath, dear,
And even so touch heaven, quite
    Sprung of its dusty atmosphere,

And casting after, stage by stage,
  Elate propellants, point afar —

If even so from earth, what span,
  Love, in ascension from a star?

FINISTERRE

And yet a kiss, like blubber, 'd blur and slip,
Without the assuring skull beneath the lip.

So the scrivener quilled. In blurry *bluh*'s, such stuff
As charading the flab of flesh, with play enough
On that *kiss* and *skull* for a high sign: love and death
— Two which, the whole world over, catch our breath.
Perpending the two, he sorts their *is*, and *has*,
With many a resonant sequitur, such as:

No way to enfold the flesh and not feel bone.
No way: kiss flesh (poor thing) and you kiss alone.
There's no one home — not a soul. Tang, gusto, glow
Carouse in the skull: heaven's carousel of snow,
Good sleighing one Christmas Eve, Ghost Lake in Maine,
And what you did, age seven, in the rain
Under the maple's tent — no sensual hour
But had its glory in the bone-built tower.

"Tower! There's your old high-horse way! Folks below
Tell: it's a tackier shanty."

                    Even so,
Celebrate — sleek or tousled, in bow, béret,
Goldenhead, towhead, chestnut, raven, grey —
All the world's flurry in your thatchy hut
(There's nothing but old foodstuff in the gut).

Lay your head closer, love. It's world on world
When lips on, up, in, under lips are curled.

Like riding the primal lava!

                    Some such flare
Rolling us, molten, to far Finisterre.
Before us, zodiacal sagas. On we grope,
To be spun in a spangling Nova — there's our hope!

To be spun, like the North's wild lovelocks, round the pole —
Space and time
                twirl immersing
                            soul in soul.

NOTES

1 This poem (the Harvard Phi Beta Kappa poem, 1978) might be described as concerned with relations between reason and imagination, fact and fable, theory and myth — *science and poetry.* And about how the view of the universe suggested by modern science is a kind of magnificent myth — or poem.

2 Stanza II. Percival Lowell (1855–1916), the brother of Amy Lowell, was the Phi Beta Kappa poet at Harvard in 1889. A writer on Japanese and Korean culture, he later devoted himself to astronomy, particularly at the Lowell Observatory at Flagstaff. He thought that the "canals" on Mars were part of an irrigation system that showed the planet was inhabited. Perturbations in the orbit of Uranus (and of Neptune) convinced him that there was a Planet X beyond them. In 1930 a planet was indeed found so close to the place he predicted that he is generally given credit for the discovery. The planet was named Pluto in his honor.

3 Stanza III. The Harvard College Observatory began, in 1875, to employ women as "computers," to study, classify, and catalogue thousands of stars from photographic plates. By 1919 forty such women had given seven hours a day, six days a week, to this highly skilled and demanding work. "Learns that *how bright* can mean *how far*" refers to Henrietta Swan Leavitt's discovery of the "period-luminosity law": her careful measurement of variable stars in the Small Magellanic Cloud suggested a correlation between true brightness and rate of variation. This was an important clue to the real distance of the star, and hence to the real size of the universe.

4 Stanza IV. Such researches as those of the Harvard women and Lowell (who seems to have worked himself into a state of nervous exhaustion) led to the view of the universe and its origin that many — probably most — scientists hold today. From the explosion of the primal fireball came (eventually) the stars whose core burned at such a temperature that thermonuclear reactions produced the elements we know. Great explosions scattered the elements into space, where (eventually!) they fell together into such galaxies and systems as our own, with the world we live in.